The Mental

by Richard Bean

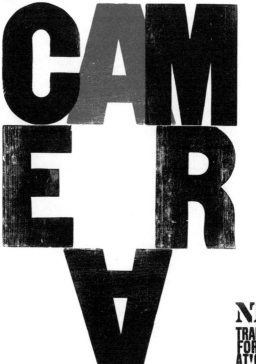

NT
TRANS
FORM
AT!ON

TRANSFORMATION

29 April–21 September 2002

The Lyttelton *Transformation* project is vital to my idea of the
National Theatre because it both celebrates and challenges our
identity. What do we want the National to be? We must draw on
our heritage, on our recent past, and on the talent of the next
generation. I want a thriving new audience, including a body
of young people under 30 with a theatre-going habit, a new
generation of artistic and administrative talent committed to
taking the National forward and a realization of the varied
potential within this glorious building.

Trevor Nunn Director of the National Theatre

Transformation is thirteen world premieres, hosted in two new
theatre spaces, with special low ticket prices. The National's most
traditional auditorium, the Lyttelton, has been transformed by
a sweep of seats from circle to stage to create a new intimacy
between actor and audience. At the same time the Loft has been
created – a fully flexible 100-seat theatre. *Transformation* will
introduce new generations of theatre makers and theatre audiences
to one of the most exciting theatres in the world.

Mick Gordon Artistic Associate
Joseph Smith Associate Producer

Transformation has received major creative input from the Studio –
the National Theatre's laboratory for new work and its engine
room for new writing – and celebrates the Studio's continuing
investment in theatre makers.

The Mentalists

by Richard Bean

In order of speaking

Ted	MICHAEL FEAST
Morrie	DUNCAN PRESTON
Woman in video footage	STYLIANI (ASTERO) LAMPRINOU

Director	SEAN HOLMES
Designer	JONATHAN FENSOM
Lighting Designer	STEVE BARNETT
Sound Designer	RICH WALSH
Company Voice Work	PATSY RODENBURG & KATE GODFREY

Production Manager	Katrina Gilroy
Stage Manager	Stuart Calder
Deputy Stage Manager	Lotte Buchan
Assistant Stage Manager	Marion Marrs
Costume Supervisor	Frances Gager
Casting	Gabrielle Dawes
Production Photographer	John Haynes

OPENING: Loft 8 July 2002

Copies of this cast list in braille or large print are available at the Information Desk

MICHAEL FEAST
TED

Michael Feast trained at the Central School of Speech and Drama. **Theatre** includes at the National: Genady in *The Forest*, Ariel in *The Tempest*, Foster in *No Man's Land*, Bobby in *American Buffalo*, Mayhew in *Dispatches*, Raymond in *Watch It Come Down*. For the RSC: Faust in *Faust 1 & 2*, the Duke in *Measure for Measure* and Becket in *Murder in the Cathedral*. At the Royal Court: Card Player in *Prairie De Chien*, John in *The Shawl*, Joe Conran in *Ourselves Alone*, the Witch in *Elizabeth I*. At Manchester Royal Exchange: Subtle in *The Alchemist*, Billy Bigelow in *Carousel*, Roland Maule in *Present Laughter*, Henry Antrobus in *Skin of Our Teeth*, Telyeghin in *Uncle Vanya*, Nick in *What the Butler Saw*. Elsewhere: Anthony Kersley QC in *The Accused* (Haymarket); Renfield in *The Passion of Dracula* (Queens); Woof in the original cast of *Hair* (Shaftesbury); Barratt in *The Servant* (Lyric, Hammersmith); Lopakhin in *The Cherry Orchard* (English Touring Company); Macheath in *The Beggar's Opera* (Wilton's Music Hall); Narrator in Prokofiev's *Romeo and Juliet* (Barbican Concert Hall); Fitzroy in *After Darwin* and Harold in *Clever Soldiers* (Hampstead); Verkhovensky in *The Possessed* (Almeida); Ivanov in *Every Good Boy Deserves Favour* (Royal Festival Hall); Jean in *Miss Julie* (Liverpool Playhouse); Mercutio in *Romeo and Juliet* (Shaw) and Scrooge in *A Christmas Carol* (Chichester). **TV** includes *The Steven Lawrence Case*, *Midsomer Murders*, *Touching Evil 1,2 & 3*, *Kavanagh QC*, *Miss Marple: a Caribbean Mystery*, *Underbelly*, *Resnick*, *Clarissa*, *Shadow of the Noose*, *Studio*, *Nightwatch*, *Blind Justice* and *Fields of Gold*. **Film** includes *Long Time Dead*, *Young Blades*, *Sleepy Hollow*, *Velvet Goldmine*, *Prometheus*, *The Tribe*, *The Fool*, *McVicar*, *The Draughtsman's Contract*, *Brother Sun Sister Moon*. Recent **Radio** includes John Osborne in *The Charge of the Light Brigade* by John Osborne, John in *Don't Look Now* by Daphne Du Maurier, Bloom in *From Here To Eternity*, Pio in *The Bridge Over The San Luis Rey* by Thornton Wilder.

DUNCAN PRESTON
MORRIE

Duncan Preston trained at RADA and began his career in rep at Sheffield followed by a tour of Europe with Ian McKellen in *Hamlet*. His other **theatre** credits include two and a half years at the RSC playing in *Romeo and Juliet*, *Macbeth*, *Pillars of the Community* and *A Midsummer Night's Dream* amongst others. He went on to play Bottom in *A Midsummer Night's Dream* at the Greek National Theatre in Athens. He played other leading parts in rep including *Little Malcolm*, *Macbeth* and Colin in *Ashes*. He appeared at Hampstead Theatre Club in Stephen Poliakoff's *Clever Soldiers* and Beth Henley's *Debutante Ball*. At the Mermaid Theatre he played Lenny in *Of Mice and Men* and Mitch in *A Streetcar Named Desire*. He played Truscott in *Loot* at Theatr Clwyd and was Big Julie in *Guys and Dolls* at the NT. His early **TV** includes *Gentry* with Roger Daltry, *Buddy*, *Holed* and 3 series of *Hunter's Walk* as PC Fred Pooley. *Happy Since I Met You* was the first time he worked with Victoria Wood which led to a 20-year association as part of her team. He was in *Victoria Wood As Seen on TV* (which included the celebrated *Acorn Antiques)*, *Wood & Walters* and *Pat and Margaret*, as well as many Victoria Wood specials. Most recently he was Stan in *Dinner Ladies*. He played Jonathan Haslam in seven series of *Surgical Spirit*, and has been seen in *Holby City*, *Midsomer Murders*, *The Bill*, *My Family*, *Heartbeat*, *Casualty*, *Peak Practice*, *Dalziel & Pascoe*, *Randall & Hopkirk (Deceased)*, *Harry Enfield Shows*, *Noah's Ark*, *Coogan's Run* and the forthcoming series *The Royal*. His **film** credits include *Porridge*, *Milk* and *A Passage to India*.

RICHARD BEAN
AUTHOR

Richard Bean was born in Hull. He first two stage plays were Toast (Royal Court) and Mr England (Sheffield Crucible), both staged as co-productions with the NT Studio. He has also written three radio plays: Of Rats and Men (Radio Four), Unsinkable (Radio Three) and Robin Hood's Revenge (Radio Four). He wrote the libretto for Stephen McNeff's opera Paradise of Fools (Unicorn Arts Theatre). He was the Pearson Bursary writer in residence at the Royal National Theatre Studio for 2001. He is the co-winner (with Gary Owen) of the George Devine Award 2002 for his play Under the Whaleback, to be produced at the Royal Court in 2003.

SEAN HOLMES
DIRECTOR

Sean Holmes' directing credits include A Midsummer Night's Dream and As You Like It (NT Education tours). For the RSC The Roman Actor, The Herbal Bed (revived for tour) and Woyzeck. Also The Contractor and Comedians (Oxford Stage Company); A Christmas Carol (Chichester Festival Theatre); In Celebration, Aristocrats, The Sea and The King of Prussia (Minerva Theatre, Chichester); The Suitcase Kid (Tricycle); Romeo and Juliet, The Power of Darkness, The Revenger's Tragedy, The Pelican, Trees Die Standing Up, A Christmas Carol, The Lesson (Orange Tree); Salt Lake Psycho (Man in the Moon).

JONATHAN FENSOM
DESIGNER

Future theatre credits include Abigail's Party (Hampstead), After the Dance (Oxford Stage Company), Dealer's Choice, My Night with Reg (Birmingham). Recent credits include So Long Life (Theatre Royal Bath & tour); Hay Fever (Oxford Stage Company); Voyzek (Birmingham Opera Co); Spike (Nuffield, Southampton); Navy Pier, Stop Kiss, Angels & Saints, Be My Baby, Soho's Season at the Pleasance (Soho); The Rivals (Northcott Exeter); Passing Places (Derby & Greenwich); Erpingham Camp (Edinburgh Assembly Rooms & tour); Alarms & Excursions (Argentina); Blithe Spirit, A Streetcar Named Desire, Richard III, Bouncers (Mercury Theatre, Colchester); East (West End & tour); Backroom (Bush); Dangerous Corner, The Government Inspector (Watermill, Newbury); Immaculate Misconception (New End Theatre); Closer than Ever (Jermyn Street Theatre); Schippel the Plumber (Palace Theatre, Watford); Take Away (Lyric Hammersmith); Richard III (Pleasance, tour to Germany); Ghetto (Riverside); Roots and Wings (Sherman Theatre); A Nightingale Sang (Nuffield, Southampton); Yusupov (Andrew Lloyd Webber's Sydmonton Festival); The Importance of Being Earnest, Billy Liar, Wait Until Dark (Salisbury Playhouse); September Tide (West End); Associate designer on Disney's The Lion King, which premiered at the new Amsterdam Theatre on Broadway and subsequently opened worldwide. TV includes tvSSFBM EHKL (A Surreal Film, Arena). Film: Tomorrow La Scala, recently shown at Cannes.

STEVE BARNETT
LIGHTING DESIGNER

Lighting credits include The Shadow of a Boy, Free, Sing Yer Heart Out for the Lads, Sparkleshark (National), Carmen and L'Elisir d'Amore (Surrey Opera), Bedroom Farce and Blithe Spirit (Redgrave Theatre), Sympathetic Magic (Finborough), La Venexiana (Etcetera) and Evelyn Glennie's multi-media show Shadow touring UK and Europe. He has worked at many regional theatres and at the National since 1994. He relit Frogs (NT Education tour) and has been Assistant to the Lighting Designer on My Fair Lady, A Winter's Tale, The Waiting Room, Mother Courage and Peter Pan, relighting the revival.

RICH WALSH
SOUND DESIGNER

Previous sound designs include: The Shadow of a Boy, Free, Sing Yer Heart Out for the Lads, The Walls (National), Exposure, Under The Blue Sky, On Raftery's Hill, Sacred Heart, Trust, Choice (Royal Court); Julie Burchill is Away (Soho Theatre); 50 Revolutions (Whitehall); The Boy Who Left Home, The Nation's Favourite (UK tours), Yllana's 666 (Riverside Studios); Strike Gently Away From Body, Blavatsky (Young Vic Studio); Body And Soul, Soap Opera, The Baltimore Waltz (Upstairs At The Gatehouse), Small Craft Warnings (Pleasance); The Taming of the Shrew, Macbeth (Japanese tour); Dirk, Red Noses (Oxford Playhouse); The Wizard of Oz, The Winter's Tale (Old Fire Station, Oxford).

The Loft Theatre was created with the help of the Royal National Theatre Foundation.

Many of the projects in the *Transformation* season were developed in the National Theatre Studio.

The Transformation season is supported by Edward and Elissa Annunziato, Peter Wolff Theatre Trust, and by a gift from the estate of André Deutsch.

ON WORD graphics designed by typographer Alan Kitching using original wood letters.

NATIONAL THEATRE BOOKSHOP
The National's Bookshop in the Main Entrance foyer on the ground floor stocks a wide range of theatre-related books. Texts of Richard Bean's *Under the Whaleback*, *Toast* and *Mr England*, of all the plays in the Loft during the Transformation season, and of the plays in *Channels (France)* including Richard Bean's translation of Serge Valletti's *Le Pub!* are available from the NT Bookshop at £2.
T: 020 7452 3456; www.nationaltheatre.org.uk/bookshop

TRANSFORMATION SEASON TEAM (Loft)
ARTISTIC ASSOCIATE Mick Gordon
ASSOCIATE PRODUCER Joseph Smith
ADMINISTRATOR Sarah Nicholson
LOFT THEATRE DESIGNER Will Bowen
FRONT OF HOUSE DESIGNER Jo Maund
FRONT OF HOUSE DESIGN PRODUCTION MANAGER Gavin Gibson
LITERARY MANAGER Jack Bradley
PLANNING PROJECT MANAGER Paul Jozefowski
RESIDENT DIRECTOR – LOFT Paul Miller
PRODUCTION CO-ORDINATOR Katrina Gilroy
PRODUCTION MANAGER – LOFT REALISATION Jo Maund
PRODUCTION ASSISTANTS – LOFT REALISATION Alan Bain and Gavin Gibson
LOFT LIGHTING REALISATION & TECHNICIANS Mike Atkinson, Steve Barnett,
Pete Bull, Huw Llewellyn, Cat Silver
LOFT SOUND REALISATION Adam Rudd, Rich Walsh
LOFT STAGE TECHNICIANS Danny O'Neill, Stuart Smith
MODEL MAKERS Aaron Marsden and Riette Hayes-Davies
GRAPHIC DESIGNERS Patrick Eley and Stephen Cummiskey
PROGRAMME EDITOR Dinah Wood
PRESS Lucinda Morrison, Mary Parker, Gemma Gibb
MARKETING David Hamilton-Peters
THEATRE MANAGER John Langley

Thanks to the following people who were part of the original Lyttelton Development Group:
Ushi Bagga, Alice Dunne, Annie Eves-Boland, Jonathan Holloway, Gareth James,
Mark Jonathan, Holly Kendrick, Paul Jozefowski, Angus MacKechnie, Tim Redfern,
Chris Shutt, Matt Strevens, Jane Suffling, Nicola Wilson, Dinah Wood, Lucy Woollatt

The National's workshops are responsible for, on these productions:
Armoury; Costume; Props & furniture; Scenic construction; Scenic Painting; Wigs

TRANSFORMATION SEASON

IN THE LYTTELTON

A co-production between the National Theatre & Théâtre National de Chaillot

The PowerBook .... 9 May–4 June
from a novel by Jeanette Winterson
devised by Jeanette Winterson, Deborah Warner & Fiona Shaw
Director Deborah Warner

A Prayer for Owen Meany .... 10–29 June
a novel by John Irving
adapted by Simon Bent
Director Mick Gordon

A collaboration between the National Theatre & Trestle Theatre Company

The Adventures of the Stoneheads .... 4–13 July
written & directed by Toby Wilsher

A collaboration between the National Theatre & Mamaloucos Circus

The Birds .... 22 July–3 August
by Aristophanes, in a new version by Sean O'Brien
Director Kathryn Hunter

Play Without Words .... 20 August–14 September
devised & directed by Matthew Bourne

IN THE LOFT

Sing Yer Heart Out for the Lads .... 29 April–15 May
by Roy Williams
Director Simon Usher

Free .... 20 May–8 June
by Simon Bowen
Director Thea Sharrock

Life After Life .... 28 May–8 June
a reportage play by Paul Jepson & Tony Parker
Director Paul Jepson

The Shadow of a Boy .... 13–29 June
by Gary Owen
Director Erica Whyman

The Mentalists .... 4–20 July
by Richard Bean
Director Sean Holmes

Sanctuary .... 25 July–10 August
by Tanika Gupta
Director Hettie Macdonald

The Associate .... 15–31 August
by Simon Bent
Director Paul Miller

Closing Time .... 4–21 September
by Owen McCafferty
Director James Kerr

NATIONAL THEATRE STUDIO &
TRANSFORMATION

All the plays in the LOFT are co-produced with the National Theatre Studio. The Studio is the National's laboratory for research and development, providing a workspace outside the confines of the rehearsal room and stage, where artists can experiment and develop their skills.

As part of its training for artists there is an on-going programme of classes, workshops, seminars, courses and masterclasses. Residencies have also been held in Edinburgh, Vilnius, Belfast and South Africa, enabling artists from a wider community to share and exchange experiences.

Central to the Studio's work is a commitment to new writing. The development and support of writers is demonstrated through play readings, workshops, short-term attachments, bursaries and sessions with senior writers. Work developed there continually reaches audiences throughout the country and overseas, on radio, film and television as well as at the National and other theatres. Most recent work includes the award-winning plays *Further than the Furthest Thing* by Zinnie Harris (Tron Theatre, Glasgow; Traverse, Edinburgh, and NT), *The Waiting Room* by Tanika Gupta (NT) and *Gagarin Way* by Gregory Burke (in association with Traverse, Edinburgh; NT; and at the Arts Theatre), *The Walls* by Colin Teevan (NT), *Accomplices* by Simon Bent, *Mr England* by Richard Bean (in association with Sheffield Theatres) and *The Slight Witch* by Paul Lucas (in association with Birmingham Rep), as well as a season of five new plays from around the world with the Gate Theatre, and *Missing Reel* by Toby Jones at the Traverse during the Edinburgh Festival 2001. *Gagarin Way* and *Further than the Furthest Thing* were part of SPRINGBOARDS – a series of partnerships created by the Royal National Theatre Studio with other theatres, enabling work by emerging writers to reach a wider audience.

Direct Action, a collaboration between The Studio and the Young Vic, is an initiative that provides young directors with an opportunity to work on the main stage of the Young Vic. Two plays were co-produced in the autumn of 2001: Max Frisch's *Andorra*, directed by Gregory Thompson; and David Rudkin's *Afore Night Come*, directed by Rufus Norris, who won the Evening Standard award for Best Newcomer for this production.

For the Royal National Theatre Studio

HEAD OF STUDIO	Sue Higginson
STUDIO MANAGER	Matt Strevens
TECHNICAL MANAGER	Eddie Keogh
INTERNATIONAL PROJECTS MANAGER	Philippe Le Moine

Royal National Theatre
South Bank, London SE1 9PX
Box Office: 020 7452 3000
Information: 020 7452 3400

Registered Charity No: 224223

The chief aims of the National, under the direction of Trevor Nunn, are to present a diverse repertoire, embracing classic, new and neglected plays; to present these plays to the very highest standards; and to give audiences a wide choice.

All kinds of other events and services are on offer – short early-evening Platform performances; work for children and education work; free live entertainment both inside and outdoors at holiday times; exhibitions; live foyer music; backstage tours; bookshops; plenty of places to eat and drink; and easy car-parking. The nearby Studio acts as a resource for research and development for actors, writers and directors.

We send productions on tour, both in this country and abroad, and do all we can, through ticket-pricing, to make the NT accessible to everyone.

The National's home on the South Bank, opened in 1976, contains three separate theatres: the Olivier, the Lyttelton, and the Cottesloe and – during *Transformation* – a fourth: the Loft. It is open to the public all day, six days a week, fifty-two weeks a year. Stage by Stage – an exhibition on the NT's history, can be seen in the Olivier Gallery.

First published in 2002 by Oberon Books Ltd.
(incorporating Absolute Classics)
521 Caledonian Road, London N7 9RH
Tel: 020 7607 3637 / Fax: 020 7607 3629

e-mail: oberon.books@btinternet.com

A catalogue record for this book is available from the British Library.

ISBN: 1 84002 287 6

Printed in Great Britain by Antony Rowe Ltd, Chippenham.

Characters

MORRIE
fifty-five

TED
fifty-five

Note

The following script was correct at the time of going to press but may differ slightly from the play as performed.

Scene 1

Summer, and a sunny day.

A bed and breakfast hotel room in Finsbury Park, London. The establishment is a poor quality, but not seedy, two or three star hotel. It has been created from two Edwardian town houses knocked together. Furniture consists of a trouser press, double bed, mini-bar, telephone etc. The door is up stage left, the double bed centre stage, and there is an en-suite bathroom just off stage right. There is a full length horizontal mirror on the wall stage right. There is a television and a telephone on a full-length-of-the-wall shelf stage right. The decor is death-defyingly bland pastel. In the back wall there is a large double sash window, which opens onto the back of the hotel and the kitchen bins. A coffee table is centre stage on which is a half full bowl of fruit. There is a double bed in the centre of the room. A foil platter of fresh sandwiches in cling film suggests someone is expected. The general state of the decor is one of worn out bland conformity in need of a clean.

Enter TED. He carries a briefcase with papers and books and a suit in a thin plastic dry cleaner's bag with wire hanger, and black business shoes. He deposits these on the stage left side of the double bed. He is wearing smart creased shorts and a white short sleeved shirt with deck shoes and no socks. He stands in the middle of the room and looks around disapprovingly with hands on hips.

TED: Typical. Tch! Look at this, eh? Morrie?!

TED sticks his head out into the corridor looking for MORRIE.

Morrie! We're in here. (*To himself.*) Daft bastard.

Enter MORRIE laden down with a video camera, box, tripod and a plastic carrier bag. He is well-kept in a mutton dressed as lamb sort of way. He wears smart, cream, chino style slacks, white shoes, and a dark, nightclub style silk shirt. His hair suffers from having had a far too trendy, spiky cut. MORRIE deposits the camera boxes on the stage right side of the bed and immediately inspects the sandwiches. TED paces about the room, looking critically, and with some disenchantment, at the space from different angles.

Bloody typical isn't it. Eh? I wanted a bigger room with two singles. Hard work moving a double. It's small. Huh, and when you want a double, you know, to sleep in – can you get one? No, you bloody can't!

MORRIE: (*Inspecting the sandwiches.*) Meat. Ted! Every single last one of them's bleeding meat.

TED: I like a bit of meat.

MORRIE: (*Lighting a cigarette.*) Bad for you matey. Kill you in the end. (*He puts the platter aside, sits on the stage right side of the bed and looks at the room.*)

Class hotel this, once. (*He stands looking for an ashtray. He finds one, puts it in the palm of his hand and sits again.*)

TED: Should've gone to that Trusthouse Forte place near Shepshed. It's shit at Shepshed, but at least it's purpose built. This is a conversion.

MORRIE: It would've been easier if you'd come and picked me up instead of me having to get a taxi.

TED: I've had a long drive as it is.

MORRIE: Did you get stuck in traffic?

TED: Me?! Na! A50, M1, A1, A10. Three hours. Huh! Nobody gets in my way when I'm driving matey.

MORRIE: Is that your car then?

TED: Company car. Couldn't exactly be the fleet manager without having a nice car myself, eh? Three litre, sixteen valve, air conditioning, walnut trim, ABS as standard, driver's airbag – the bloody lot. It's not a Cavalier.

MORRIE: What's ABS?

TED: ABS. It's a braking system. They test the car in Iceland. Drive it about on glaciers, and bloody hell mate, that, that is *the* place to test a motor. You see, if an elk jumps out on you when you're cornering on ice at fifty you've got to have ABS brakes or you'd total the elk, total the car, and kill yourself into the bargain.

MORRIE: Why do the elks jump out at the cars?

TED: Instinct matey. Fucking instinct.

MORRIE: Do they hide in the bushes, waiting?

TED: I'm not an expert.

MORRIE: Why do they do it?

TED: It'll be a territorial thing. (*He sits on the bed, picks up the instructions on how to dial out, and dials.*) Service. It's a dirty word in this country. You go to America, ha! – anything you want – and! – with a smile, and a 'have a nice day'. And you know what?

MORRIE: What's that china?

TED: They bloody well mean it! (*On the phone.*) Denise, hello it's me, Ted, I thought you might be at lunch, well I'll just leave a message, I'm in Exeter. Er…that's about it, actually, nothing more to say. Exeter. Bye. (*He puts the phone down.*)

MORRIE: You're in Finsbury Park Ted. London, N5.

TED: (*He taps the side of his nose smugly.*) I know. (*He manhandles MORRIE gently sideways, and walks to the window. He opens it and looks out as if checking his car. Satisfied, he closes the window and then runs his wet finger along the sill.*)

(*Showing his finger.*) Look at that. Filth. Switzerland, that's another one. Tch! You can eat your breakfast off the streets. You know what? You're not allowed to have a shit after twelve o'clock at night in Switzerland. Not if you live in a block of flats. You'd get arrested. Too much noise you see. Ha! They don't bloody mess about like we do. You don't see anyone begging, nobody starving. There was a beggar outside here, sitting there with his mutt, he said, 'Have you got any spare change?' – I said, 'Of course I bloody have,' and walked on. Huh, you'd have given him money I suppose?

MORRIE: If I'd have had any I would. There but for the grace of God go I.

TED: Still a bloody commie eh? Ha!

MORRIE: International socialist. Though it's a private thing nowadays. Family tradition.

TED: (*Laughing.*) Family?!

MORRIE: My old dad was an anti-fascist.

TED: Yeah, yeah. Look at the state of this place!

MORRIE: My friend Andreas, his brother's got a hotel in Cyprus, Larnaca, very reasonable prices. I stayed there three weeks. I was a virtual prisoner I was. Took all my money off me, three hundred quid, missed my flight three times. Mind you, I could have a woman any time I wanted.

TED: Vagrants? They're laughing at us matey.

MORRIE follows TED about the room all the time smoking and holding his ashtray in his hand.

MORRIE: My old dad designed the perfect murder, which involved the use of a wino.

TED: You told me Morrie, you told me a thousand times.

MORRIE: It's only any good if you want to kill those you live with.

TED: (*Turns and faces MORRIE.*) I know your dad's plan like the back of my hand, now can we stop pratting about and make this film?

MORRIE gets on with setting up the camera, TED with emptying his case of papers which he lays out in order on the bed.

Pause.

MORRIE: You need a wino what no-one's gonna miss. 'Bout your own age, and much the same size.

TED: Morrie!

MORRIE: You bang 'em on the head and take 'em back to your place, dress 'em in your gear, 'ang him up like he's hung himself. Kill the wife and kids then torch the house, petrol – whatever, but do a good job, especially on the wino, and then fuck off. The Old Bill will think you've topped the family and then, full of whatsaname…

TED: Remorse.

MORRIE: – remorse, you've been and gone and topped yourself, so they stop looking for you. The perfect crime.

TED: (*Without interest.*) Did he ever do it?

MORRIE: We'll never know.

Beat.

You have to have false teeth or it's no good. You take your false teeth out and stuff them...

TED: Morrie will you shutup! I'm sick of hearing about it!

Beat.

It's a bloody pipe dream Morrie.

MORRIE: I never said it was easy.

TED sits on the bed deep in thought.

Can we sort the money out first china?

TED: Sure. I'm sorry. Long drive. It's good to see you again matey. Brings it all back, eh. Good times, bloody good times.

MORRIE: Ted?

TED: What do you think is fair compensation?

MORRIE: Fifty quid?

TED: Fifty. It's a deal. (*He walks past MORRIE to end up down stage right looking towards the door up stage left.*)

MORRIE: Any chance of...

TED: Set up here I think.

MORRIE has moved to down stage right.

MORRIE: Here?

TED: (*Indicating a chair near the door.*) Yeah, I'll sit over there.

MORRIE: You're going to sit over there are you?

TED: Yeah.

MORRIE: That means, you're going to see the door as background, cinematically.

TED: (*Moves to stand in front of the door.*) It's not a bad door.

MORRIE: It's alright.

TED: Couldn't be bloody wood though, could it. Tch! Do you know what that is Morrie?

MORRIE: 'Course it's wood.

TED: Veneer. Tch! What's happened here is – they've gone and got a photographer to take a picture of a nice looking bit of maple wood and then with some glue they've stuck the ensuing photograph on some piece of old shite chipboard, and they've got the nerve to call it a hotel door. Whereas Morrie, the door I want, the door I deserve, is the door they subsequently make out of the nice looking bit of maple wood after they've got tired of taking photographs of it. That door! The maple wood door, that is MY fucking door!

MORRIE: You never change do you. Look at you. You've gone and got yourself emotionally involved with a bleeding door.

TED: I've accepted the door! It's shit, the room's shit, everything's shit, but I'm not gonna bring unnecessary tension to an already tense situation.

MORRIE: I'm not tense. Nothing wrong with the door... unless someone opens it.

TED: I told reception that we're not to be disturbed. The three Ps. Planning, Preparation, and...fuck.

MORRIE: Does she know what we're doing?

TED: She knows we're filming, yeah.

MORRIE: Does she know what?

TED: No. Nobody knows.

MORRIE goes into the en-suite bathroom. TED sits on the stage left side of the bed and takes his shorts and deck shoes off. He is now only wearing underpants.

MORRIE: (*Off.*) You couldn't pay me now could you china? I'm out of pocket.

TED: Look! I'll sort you out at the end of the day. You're not going anywhere are you. I've got sandwiches in.

MORRIE: (*Off.*) They're all meat.

We hear a tap turned on and then off. A second tap is then turned on and then off.

(*Off.*) Both taps work. I like this. An en-suite bathroom.

(*He sticks his head out as if he has something important to say.*) Tiles are good for bathrooms aren't they?

(*Off.*) I was going to have an en-suite put into my place, but the bedroom didn't have any plumbing.

(*Stands in the doorway of the en-suite and addresses TED.*)
Patrick said – do you know Patrick?

TED: Patrick? No.

MORRIE: Ex-copper. Very wiry hair.

TED: (*Manhandles MORRIE aside from the bathroom door.*)
Come on matey I need a piss.

MORRIE: He said I could fit me one of those whoosh
toilet whatsanames. You know, it chews it up like a
food mixer and whooshes it down the pipe so you only
need really thin pipes. But he said he'd have to mount
the pipes on top of the architrave and I didn't like the
idea of that. All that mashed up crap charging round
the room. It'd be like living in the middle of Ben Hur.

Beat.

Am I putting you off? Put a tap on. I find that helps.

TED: What?

MORRIE: I don't have that problem much myself, but
I could never piss next to my old dad.

TED: Ha! You're a card!

MORRIE: He took us all to Whipsnade Zoo once and
I had to stand next to him and it was just a big trough,
you know, no dividers, and he had a big one. Biggest
one I've ever seen, like a baby's arm holding an apple,
and I was only six, and I couldn't go.

TED: You and your bloody dad!

MORRIE: Later on I wet myself in the reptile house.
Nobody noticed. It's usually alright, isn't it, you know if
you're dying to go, but it's when you just want to do a

21

clever one, and someone's there watching, though they're never really watching, it's just that they can tell. That's the sort of vision what made Bobby Charlton so exceptional. Whatsaname vision they call it.

TED: Peripheral vision.

MORRIE: That's it.

TED: What a player eh! These kids today they couldn't hold a candle!

MORRIE: Jackie Charlton was handy in a different sort of way, but he never had the same peripheral vision.

Pissing is heard.

That's it. Go on my son. Yes, if you were standing next to Bobby Charlton trying to have a piss you'd have a bit of a problem. But next to Jackie, it'd be alright, although he's a big chap Jackie so there's always the chance you might feel er...whatsaname –

Pause.

TED: (*From the bathroom.*) Intimidated.

MORRIE: (*Standing, excited by the revelation.*) Hey, Ted! If Jackie had had Bobby's peripheral vision, you wouldn't have stood a chance, not in a urinal without dividers.

Beat.

Me? I always go before I leave home.

The toilet flushes. TED reappears and heads straight for the bed, sitting with his back to MORRIE on the stage left side. He now begins to dress, putting on a clean white, business style shirt and tie.

TED: No socks! Bloody hell! Brain dead!

MORRIE: You can borrow mine. They're not mine as a matter of fact. They belong to Andreas. Did I tell you about Andreas? He killed six Turks one night. What he does is, he talks to them, plays cards, then when they're not looking he slits their throats.

TED checks himself out in the mirror. Then, happy with the look of the shirt, goes back to sitting on the stage left side of the bed. MORRIE follows him, continuing his story. TED puts his suit jacket on.

TED: How are you getting on with that camera?

MORRIE: He was the first minder you know. People used to say to him, 'What do you do Andreas?' and he used to say, 'I'm a minder,' and of course no-one knew what the fuck he was talking about. Not until Minder came out on the telly that is, and then, of course everyone knew what he did, though it's not at all like it is on the telly. He minds for this crippled bloke in a wheelchair. Gets money from the government for it…can you believe it?

TED: I have no bloody difficulty believing that. We give it away mate.

MORRIE: I didn't believe it either, but he doesn't like being questioned. He nearly went into one, he did, and then the next day, what does he do? Wheels the bloody cripple into the shop, and says, 'There you are Morrie, now do you believe me?' He wheels the cripple round all of his Cypriot coffee houses, and the cripple's not even a member, he's not even bleeding Cypriot. He's got it all wrong, that Andreas. He thinks he's walking a bleeding dog. Andreas has got a Cavalier.

TED goes over to the mirror to put his tie on. MORRIE breaks off from setting up the camera and stands behind TED talking to his reflection in the mirror.

I don't have a car. What do I need a car for? My daughter lives in Australia.

TED: (*Becoming impatient.*) Look...!

MORRIE: – if I'd known that that woman I married, was the sort of woman who'd secretly do the lottery, win the jackpot, and then fuck off to Australia with my only daughter I would never have walked down that aisle.

TED: Morrie!

MORRIE: If I had a son, I'd teach him to be selfish. Look at me. Give, give, give fucking give. Father Christmas I am. Yeah, and nobody gives a fuck about him. Not until December. You can wear my socks.

TED: My feet will be out of shot, won't they?

MORRIE: Depends on what you're planning to do with them.

TED: What?

MORRIE: If they're going to feature, then you'll need socks.

TED: Why would I want my feet to feature?

MORRIE: I don't know. I don't know what you want me to do.

TED: (*Assertively.*) Look, I don't want you to do anything clever, nothing bloody artistic alright? Just set the thing going and leave it, yeah?

MORRIE: Alright, alright.

Pause.

I could pan in and out every now and then to make it a bit more interesting.

TED: Just get the sound right and leave it matey. Okay!

MORRIE: (*Petulant.*) I don't know why you need me here.

TED: Oh I'm sorry. Good of you to help out. I knew you would. You're reliable. A real pal. It's good to see you.

There is a polite knock at the door. TED freezes. MORRIE starts heading towards the door but TED grabs him by the shoulder.

MORRIE: What's up?

TED: Don't fucking move!

MORRIE: Why not? It might be some different sandwiches.

TED: (*Whispered.*) Be quiet!

MORRIE: Have you invited anyone to watch?

TED: Watch what?

MORRIE: I don't know. I don't know what you're gonna do. It might be worth watching.

There is a second knock. They don't move.

Why don't you let them in?

TED: (*A fierce whisper.*) Shutup!

TED covers MORRIE's mouth with his hand. A note is pushed under the door. TED stops and stares and

then picks up the note. Inside the note is a credit card. He
then opens the door, steps into the corridor and steps back
into the room.

No-one there. (*He reads the note, throws the credit card onto*
the bed.)

MORRIE: Not good eh?

TED: Bloody card's bounced. (*He goes into his wallet and*
finds another credit card. He picks up the phone, and dials
reception.)

MORRIE: What was all that about? You'll have cash for
me? Today?

TED: Shhhhh! (*On the phone.*) Hello, Edward Oswald
room three, one, four... Yeah...well I'm totally
amazed. I bought petrol with it this morning... Yeah...
have you godda pen?... Five, four, three, four, two, six,
seven, zero zero zero zero zero three, four, eight, three
expiry date, four, two thousand and one... What do
you need that for?... This is incredible, I mean it's a
forty quid room, I'm not buying a bloody yacht...
Edward Oswald... Oswald, like Oswald Mosley... It's
a company credit card. Sumners Industrial,
Loughborough.

MORRIE: Easy!

TED: (*He puts the phone down.*) Never heard of Oswald
Mosley. What do they teach them in school eh? How to
inject heroin, that's what.

MORRIE: I don't want a cheque. I'm in the middle of a
correspondence with the bank.

TED: Cash. At the end of the day. Trust me.

*MORRIE goes back to setting the video up. TED takes his
shoes off, troubled by the sock problem. Then he puts his
trousers on, and after that, the shoes, again with no socks.
He then goes to the chair and sits on it with his briefcase on
his lap. He takes papers from the briefcase and puts them on
the edge of the bed. Amongst these papers is an old, tatty,
hardback novel.*

MORRIE: Do you know what you're going to say?

TED: I've got it written down.

MORRIE: You're not going to read it though are you?

TED: No, I don't think so.

MORRIE: Good. Nothing worse, and you're not a natural
communicator. My old dad was a good speaker. Used
to have 'em there, in the palm of his hand. Jokes –
he was a professional comedian at one time, but he
didn't like smoking. He could sing too. He played
professional cricket as well. He hit six sixes in one
over, that was before that Gary Sobers did it. But
no-one took any notice. Oh yes he could sing. That's
how he met my mother.

TED: (*Without interest.*) How is she?

MORRIE: (*Stops working and comes to the middle of the
room.*) She's dead.

TED: Is she? Bloody hell. Did I know that?

MORRIE: Yes, you did.

TED: Did you kill her?

Beat.

You always said you'd kill her – if you had to.

MORRIE: She was my own mother.

TED: Yes, I know, but you told me that if it had to be done…

MORRIE: She died in a car crash. She died a natural death.

TED: I'm sorry.

Silence.

Were you driving?

MORRIE: I don't have a bleeding car! Haven't you been listening?

TED: Who was driving then?

MORRIE: Bloke from the council. He was bringing her to see me. Hit by a sodding fire engine they were.

TED: Did you get to meet her then?

MORRIE: Na. They wanted me to go and identify the body being the next of kin, but I said I'd never met her – which of course is true, sort of.

TED: Bloody hell, you didn't tell me – I'd have remembered that.

MORRIE: I told you. You forgot 'cos you don't give a fuck and you eat too much meat.

TED: I liked the old gal.

MORRIE: You never met her.

TED: What I mean is – I liked the sound of her, what you'd told me about her.

MORRIE: I made that up, didn't I?

MORRIE goes back to setting the camera. He puts a tape in it. TED starts writing notes.

TED: (*Head down.*) Your dad's dead isn't he? I'm clear on that. Kaw! Only he could go out like that. Mind you, a fire engine comes close.

MORRIE: I think he planned it like that. He was a hard man.

TED: Ugh! I don't like to think about it Morrie. It gives me the willies. Ugh!

MORRIE: Like a god he was. He had a chest like a spare bed.

TED: You were a bit of a disappointment for him weren't you matey?

MORRIE: (*Leaves the camera and approaches TED.*) He told me straight. He said to me when I left school he said, 'Morrie, hairdressing's a puff's game.'

TED: You told me.

MORRIE: Even when I was in the World Championships in Soho that time, he could've come and watched but he went and played snooker instead.

TED: Let it go matey! It'll eat away at you. Have you got that thing tested yet?

MORRIE: Getting there. (*He moves back to the camera.*) I've made a lot of the films with this one. Not bad quality is it?

TED: Did you do the balloon one with that camera?

MORRIE: What was her name? There's balloons in a few of them.

TED: I can't remember her name.

MORRIE: They always say their names at the beginning. Though it's never their real names of course. Got to protect their whatsaname.

TED: Anonymity. I never have the sound on.

MORRIE: You what?

TED: I never have the bloody sound on! (*He puts his case on the bed and stands, yawns with nerves, and rubs his face.*)

MORRIE: Well if you knew how much work I put into getting the sound right you'd listen out of respect for me – if nothing else.

TED: I'm not sure about this no socks business.

MORRIE: Do the shoes pinch?

TED: They do a bit.

MORRIE: Don't wear them then.

TED: (*Sits and takes his shoes off.*) It's what it's gonna look like, though. Some top people are gonna be ringing up for this one. I'm not trying to attract your usual half educated orang-utan.

TED stands and goes over to the camera, and moves MORRIE to one side so that he can look through the lens.

Ha! You've come a long way with your photography haven't you Morrie. Do you remember that first picture you sent in to that porni mag? Ha! I still laugh at that. A bloody milk bottle!

MORRIE: (*Goes to sit on the chair.*) Ten quid I got for that wasn't it?

30

TED: Sit over there will you Morrie. I couldn't believe they printed it. Only Maurice Calvert would think of sticking his knob in a milk bottle.

MORRIE: I get a lot of good ideas. (*He goes to sit on the chair.*)

TED: Looks okay this. To me.

MORRIE: (*Indicating the pine door behind him.*) That wood looks alright doesn't it? I like pine.

TED: Bloody hell! How many times do I have to tell you? It's veneer.

MORRIE: Mahogany's too dark. If you get a young girl, and take her back, it puts them off if you've got a dirty great mahogany wardrobe looming over the business. Depresses them. Reminds them of their parents' bedrooms. Yeah, I like a light pine. I bet you've got pine haven't you? You and Kathy up there in Ashby de la Zouch. I don't honestly think I could get it up in a room where there was a lot of mahogany.

TED: Is the sound alright on that thing?

MORRIE goes back to the camera. TED sits in the chair.

MORRIE: I usually put the sound on later. But this is different. Say something.

TED: (*After coughing.*) Good afternoon.

Pause.

MORRIE: Keep going.

TED: What do you want me to talk about?

31

MORRIE: What did you have for breakfast?

TED: I didn't have any breakfast.

MORRIE: Well count then.

TED: Right!

Beat.

One, two, three, four, five, six, seven…

MORRIE: Bit louder.

TED: (*Louder.*) One, two, three, four, five, six, seven…

MORRIE: That's too loud.

TED: (*Somewhere in between.*) One, two, three, four, five, six…

MORRIE: (*Presses record on the camera.*) I've started it.

TED: It's recording?

MORRIE: Yeah.

TED: Can you see my feet?

MORRIE: No. It goes down to half way up your shin.

TED: Right. (*He leans over to the bed and picks up a sheaf of papers from which he starts to read.*)

(*Reading.*) War, pollution, bigotry, over population, interpersonal violence…

MORRIE: – You're reading!

TED: Yes, yes. Right, okay. You're right. It won't work like that will it, no.

MORRIE: It looks terrible.

TED: Right! Okay. Do you want to wind the tape back and I'll try again?

MORRIE: That's not a problem.

TED: Sorry, matey, I'm just a bit nervous. It's just that this is going out to ten thousand people. Will you have enough tapes?

MORRIE: Tapes are not a problem. I know this bloke in Notting Hill, he used to be a wrestler...

TED: Great! Good, I knew I could rely on you. Some people you can rely on, and some fuck you about, but you, you...

MORRIE: Rolling!

TED: Pollution, starvation, poverty, personal crime, bad language in public places, war. These are a few of the things which have made me personally, in my own life...

The phone rings.

Oh fuck!!

(*Picks up the phone and answers it.*) What?... It's a company credit card...have Sumners gone bust while I've been sitting here? (*He gets up and searches for his wallet.*)

MORRIE: That's two now.

TED: Tell me about it.

TED finds his wallet and takes from it a smaller credit card concertina wallet which he flicks out to unfold it revealing about twenty-five other cards. He says nothing but raises his eyebrows mischievously at MORRIE as the cards unfold.

What do you want? A blue one, a red one, a bloody goldfish?... Alright four, nine, one zero zero zero four, five, two, three, four, six, six, five four, three, expiry seven, two thousand and two... Ring straight back alright! (*He puts the phone down.*)

MORRIE: That's a good one is it?

TED: They're all bloody good ones. Let's get something to eat.

TED picks up the platter of sandwiches from the side and puts it on the coffee table. They both sit on the end of the bed. TED tucks into the food furiously. MORRIE doesn't eat and looks straight ahead.

Not eating?

MORRIE: I'm sick of food.

Beat.

Will this one go through?

TED: (*With a full mouth.*) 'Course it bloody will! Trust me. Tch!

MORRIE: No breakfast eh?

TED: No time mate.

MORRIE: What – Kath let you out the house without a breakfast? That's not like the Kath I know.

TED: She's in Bridlington. At her sister's.

MORRIE: What's the matter Ted, nervous?

TED: Public speaking. I'd rather jump out of a fucking aeroplane.

MORRIE: (*Stands and opens the mini-bar.*) Beer?

TED: Champion.

MORRIE pours a beer and prepares himself a Bacardi and coke.

I didn't know what to talk about a minute ago, you know – testing the sound. Ha, I could never have been a barber, eh matey?

MORRIE: Very true. What people don't understand, is that your barber is your friend and your confidant. Talking, always having something to say, is as much a skill as your styling. Talking...styling. Two skills, one job. Shoulda charged twice as much. Which is why I kept my customers even after my hands went. They came to listen. (*He holds up a shaking right hand.*)

TED: Who cut the hair then?

MORRIE: Cetin. Have you met Cetin?

TED: I don't know which is he?

MORRIE: Young lad. They like me, young people. I keep myself young, you see, mentally.

TED: Yeah, you like people, don't you. Me, I'm not so keen. I wish she'd bloody ring. How long's it take to do a card?

MORRIE: Every person is like a new book. A book you haven't read. Funny innit how me, who don't like reading, likes people, and you who does like reading, don't like anyone. I liked having a shop. New people every day. Maybe a fuck.

TED: Maurice Calvert! You don't change, do you?

MORRIE: The last girl I had, Katrina, she'd set herself up in the shop doing these oil paintings of people she saw in magazines. Painted me a few times. Nude, of course. You see, I don't have a problem with that.

TED: Ha! I know that much!

MORRIE: I've got quite a good body for my age. And she liked that. I helped that girl in many ways you know. Her father had played with her you see...

TED: You're kidding!

MORRIE: She'd not been able to do it for years, but I helped her back into it. I'm gentle you see. Some blokes with a young girl are like a bull at a gate, but me I take my time, talk, massage the scalp. Do you want a scalp massage now Ted? Calm your nerves.

TED: (*Looks at his watch.*) Not right now. Katrina eh?

MORRIE: Yeah, she did two films for me. A natural actress, and very comfortable with the camera. Not at first, obviously, after what her dad had done, but after she knew she could trust me, bleeding hell, you couldn't stop her. In a previous life she'd been an aviator – female aviator. She's whatsanamed the globe.

TED: Circumnavigated?

MORRIE: No. The Globe Cinema, down Lea Bridge Road. She's done it up.

TED: Renovated?

MORRIE: Yeah. She sells carpets in it now.

TED: Are you still seeing her?

MORRIE: Her husband's got a court order out on me.

TED: Bloody hell!

MORRIE: He came in the shop and went into one. He'd set her up in a flat off Stamford Hill you see, on the game, you know, and had started smacking her about a bit, so when he came into the shop I let him have it. (*Stands and demonstrates his attack.*)

I feinted with the left and followed up with an uppercut right, came in with the left knee, and then chopped down on his head with the left. He was on the floor begging for mercy in five seconds. I had a new customer in at the time. It must have looked terrible. Ha! That lad thought he'd sort out an old man, but he didn't know about my dad, and what he'd passed on.

TED: (*Stands and picks up the phone but doesn't dial. He's restless, frustrated.*) Terrific boxer your dad.

MORRIE: (*Sits back down.*) He was the only British boxer to have boxed at every weight. He could put it on, lose it, and then put it on again. Chips.

TED: They don't make them like that anymore. What is taking so long! Come on!

MORRIE: He invented the mini skirt my dad – did you know?

TED: Here we go.

MORRIE: He'd have been rich, he would, but he made the fatal mistake of inviting Mary Quant to one of his parties. Eileen was the first girl ever to wear a mini-skirt.

TED: Oh Eileen eh! Kaw! She was a bit special eh!

MORRIE: She was in love with me.

TED: I know.

MORRIE: She didn't like sex though. Not with me anyway. She's my only failure. Girls have always liked me. I must put them at their ease. Touching people. Running a car fleet it's probably not the same is it?

TED: (*Looks at his watch, stands and paces about.*) Different world. Physical contact like that would be frowned upon.

MORRIE: It's about trust. If you start with a warm wash of the hair and a gentle scalp massage, – you're home. Obviously, if you then go and lop off a load of hair willy nilly you're not going to do yourself any favours but as long as what you do is not a million miles away from a recognisable style you can move it on a stage, because you've got their trust. But that trust can be abused. I should know I've done it a few times.

TED: With all that talent around, I don't know why you bothered getting married. (*Sits down again.*) Oh come on!

MORRIE: I thought it was love.

TED: Fag.

MORRIE gives him a cigarette, takes one for himself and lights them both.

MORRIE: I've completely forgiven her. But she took my little princess. The bitch.

TED: Yeah.

MORRIE: I never loved her. She took the poor child away before she knew the difference between right and wrong. There's only one sort of love. Your love for your own blood, your offsprings. There is no love between a man and a woman. I don't miss her. Why do I want to see her? I'm getting enough young ones, always did. Ah, fuck 'em.

TED: (*Bangs his fist against the wall.*) Why hasn't she bloody rung! (*He rings reception.*)

They're not answering.

Beat.

They're not picking it up!

Beat.

They want me to stew on it, don't they.

Beat.

They're playing games with us.

MORRIE: Maybe it's gone through.

TED: Yeah! That's it. Okay let's crack on. (*Phone down.*)

MORRIE: You ready china?

TED: I look alright, yeah?

MORRIE: Yeah. Tip. This is what they do at the BBC. Imagine you're talking to someone, one single, individual person, sitting there, in their own living room, in their favourite chair.

Beat.

Rolling.

MORRIE sets the video rolling and leaves it and TED to their own devices. He goes over to the mirror and plucks out a nasal hair, checks himself over, then sits and lights a cigarette. He pays little attention to what TED is talking about, having heard it all before, and begins – towards the end of the speech to nod off. TED's speech is interrupted with nervous coughs at first and desperate pauses, but then he flows and is unstoppable.

TED: War, poverty, corruption, spiralling taxes, bad behaviour, inter personal violence, and over-population. Do these things worry you? I think they do. They worry me too. Like you, I've probably tried meditation, alternative foods, even Buddhism for a couple of weeks. They didn't work did they? That's why you answered my ad in the national press, and that's why you're watching this video now, in your front room, in your favourite armchair. Hello. My name's Edward Oswald, Ted. I'm a fleet manager with Sumners Industrial Cleaning Products out of Loughborough, but that's not important right now, it's not the whole of me. I'm here to tell you that there's no need to change human nature in order to end inhumanity and injustice. Being inhumane, unjust, wasteful and destructive is not something people 'are' it's something people 'do'. That's right, it's behaviour. But let's start at the beginning, because I godda feeling that I'm asking you to run here before you can walk. The story for me begins at twenty-three, Wharfedale Road, Chingford, London, England, the home of my mother-in-law number one, Elizabeth Rose Dexter. My son of that time, by my first marriage – obviously, Mathew Oswald, was knocking down her garden shed and in amongst the rubbish and ruin of that shed he found a book. Not just any ordinary book, but a book that has changed my life, and could change your lives.

He reaches out to the bed and picks up a hard back novel.

Walden Two by Bhurrus Frederick Skinner. Now, the
interesting thing about Fred Skinner is that he's not a
writer, he's not even a novelist. He's a psychologist,
was a psychologist – forgive me – he's dead now. And
he's not just any tin pot, sex mad pervert psychologist
like most of the psychologists you've probably heard
of, but is, was, being dead now, unfortunately, like
I said. Huh, if he was still alive. Ah well, only the good
die young, though in fact he was seventy, actually. Just
an expression. Fred Skinner could have been, possibly
the most influential psychologist on earth, ever.
Skinner was pretty down on all the other psychologists.
He called them the Mentalists, because of their totally
misguided obsession with the mind, a line of scientific
enquiry which has never produced anything of any
use whatsoever, well nothing your average dinner
lady couldn't work out for herself anyway. But the
disgusting and unbelievable thing about the Mentalists,
and I'm talking here about Sigmund Freud and all his
junkie mates, cos he was a junkie, let's face it, cocaine,
that's well known, and all the other Mentalists of the
nineteenth century, er…sorry twentieth century, yeah,
always get that wrong, ha! where was I? er…that whole
century was ruined because of Mentalist thinking, and
Mentalist influenced policies. Look, I'll try and make
this clear. The Mentalists were only interested in the
mind, they didn't give a monkey's about behaviour,
and that's where the whole century went down the
pan. Think about it, if you're sitting on a bus you don't
give a damn what the bloke next to you is thinking
about, do you? It's what he's doing with his hands that
makes you nervous. Mind/behaviour. Two different
kettles of fish. Freud's main contribution to the

destruction of our society was that personality is fixed.
'Course, that's the perfect excuse for every criminally
inclined retard. 'I steal cars, murder and rape old age
pensioners because my cat died during the anal stage' –
the kid's anal stage, that is – not the cat's, that would be
silly. Do you see? Of course you do. But Skinner, thank
God, ignored the mind and looked at behaviour, and
dedicated his lifetime to working with rats and pigeons,
and writing down the rules of behaviour modification.
These rules, these jewels, are explained in Walden Two.
He's given us a gift, you a gift, a way of living which is
non-destructive, based on community, and fulfilling.
How does that sound? Interested? Of course you are.
Skinner discovered that behaviour could be controlled
by the design of the environment, rewards and
punishments. That lousy, anti-social behaviour could be
gotten rid of, and good, useful behaviour could be
encouraged, so that every member of that designed
community could be happy. Ask yourself – are you
happy? Are you truly happy? How happy has that new
car made you? Mmm? So, you went to B&Q and spent
thousands on a new kitchen. And did that make you
happy? Did it change your life? No, it changed your
kitchen, and there's a difference. I recently visited a
radical community in Peru, on the north west side of
that wonderful country and stayed at a Walden Two
community. I found people there successfully applying
the principles of radical behavioural psychology to
create an environment where good behaviour was
rewarded and lousy, selfish, anti-social behaviour was
punished. And, believe you me, it was working. I had
the best two months of my life before I had to leave
because of a minor misunderstanding, mainly the result

of a language problem. What I say is if a bunch of foreigners can do it, why can't we? Let me make this crystal clear. In Walden Two…

MORRIE finally drops off to sleep. TED leaps to his feet and jumps onto the bed.

Bloody hell!

MORRIE: (*Leaping up in fear.*) What's happened?

TED: I said …bloody hell!

MORRIE: What's happening?

TED: You're bloody happening that's what's bloody happening.

MORRIE: Eh?

TED backs MORRIE up to the mirror stage right.

TED: You just sat there, in full view, and fell asleep on me. I'm not very good at this. I mean, how's that supposed to make me feel eh?

MORRIE: Well I have heard it all before china. There's nothing new is there?

TED: Yes there is as a matter of fact. I was just getting to that bit.

MORRIE: Well you could've woken me up for that. I wouldn't have minded.

TED: That's not the point is it! Look this is difficult for me. Some people…some of the people I've spoken to about this treat me, well you know, you can feel them pushing you away, keeping their distance, like they're dealing with a bloody headcase or something. They're polite, oh yes, most of them, but the way they talk to you is different. I've put in a lot of time and bloody effort into this…

MORRIE: I've cancelled an appointment.

TED: You've postponed an appointment. You'll be cutting his hair tomorrow or some other day.

MORRIE: Her hair.

TED: Who's she then?

MORRIE: Consuella. She comes from Mexico. She lives in Stamford Hill. I was going to go round during her siesta.

TED: Have you met her?

MORRIE: (*Relaxes and sits on the end of the bed.*) Oh yes. She's a beautiful girl, you know in that Mexican sort of way they have.

TED: Raven black hair?

MORRIE: She's blonde now after the last time I saw her but she does have dark skin.

TED: I'm sorry mate. I thought people would be interested, you know…and they're not. Real happiness. Ha! And no-one's bloody interested! (*He sits on the end of the bed next to MORRIE.*)

MORRIE: Well, you're asking people to give up their lives, everything they've got, and go and live with you. It's a bit of a wrench.

TED: I'm asking them, initially, to give up twenty-nine ninety-nine. Thirty quid for a ticket to paradise. That matey, in anyone's book, is cheap.

MORRIE: And you want a thousand people?

TED: I need a thousand to set up the community, but more than a thousand will ring up. I'm confident of that.

MORRIE: That's a lot of money, isn't it.

TED: Minimum twenty-nine thousand nine hundred and ninety pounds. Enough to get started.

MORRIE: They might have thirty quid, but I don't know about giving everything up.

TED: Most people don't have anything to give up. Things. That's all they've got. That's not living that's... storekeeping.

MORRIE: Most people are happy doing that.

TED: (*Leaping up. Uncontrollably.*) No they're not! That's the whole fucking point!

MORRIE: No need to go into one! This is so like you. Going into one for nothing.

TED: (*Going into one.*) I am not going into one!

MORRIE: What's that then if it's not going into one?

TED: I'm just sick and tired of people treating me like a bloody headbanger. I can't tell you how exciting this is.

MORRIE: People don't like cults.

TED: Ah! Now, you're bang bloody spot on there. All those lefty bollocks 'end of the world', woo woo, ra ra, sex twenty-four hours a fucking day societies. I come along wanting to set up a community based on cleanliness, good behaviour, and sleeping with your own wife, and it's too late. Someone's already had a shit on the patio.

Beat.

Morrie?

MORRIE: Yeah.

TED: Are you alright in the maisonette? On your own?

MORRIE: I don't miss her. This bloke Bob's started coming round. Stays in the spare room sometimes. Uninvited. He thinks I'm Ralph. You know Ralph, used to be a trackside marshal at the Speedway. Bob's making a terrible mistake, but he's good company. Saws a lot. Wood.

TED: I need a thousand people. You could be one of the first. A planner.

MORRIE: 'Course. In there like a shot. You get it set up china. A thousand new people. Keep me amused that would.

TED: You're a pal. I'm sorry I lost it earlier.

MORRIE: You're a passionate man. Now, why don't we start again and maybe I'll do a bit of camera work, you know, zoom in and out a bit, break it up for the punters.

TED: Right. Good idea, matey.

MORRIE: Go and wash your face, you look like a kid.

TED goes to the bathroom. As MORRIE changes tapes, he lights a cigarette and checks his watch.

TED: (*Off.*) This is the future you know. The next century is gonna be about personal action. Politics, in the sense of voting for someone, is dead and bloody buried mate. They're all the same. If you want to change the world you do your own thing.

(*Appearing, rubbing his face with a towel.*) I just want taking seriously, that's all. Sometimes I lie awake and I can see the community, a thousand people, happy, well behaved, you know, clean.

MORRIE: In the country?

TED: Ah! Doesn't have to be. That's a common mistake of the romantic elements of your lefty communities. They all wanted to get into farming 'cos of all the spirituality crap about getting close to the earth, but when push came to shove, none of them had the bollocks to kill the chicken for tea. Consequently they spent all their time sitting around eating omelettes, getting depressed. Bingo – community fails.

MORRIE: I don't eat meat.

Footsteps are heard outside in the corridor.

TED: Shhh!!!

TED listens to the footsteps. They stop outside the door. TED goes to listen at the door. He presses his ear against the door.

MORRIE: What –

TED: Shhhhh!!!!!!

TED listens for a few moments. The footsteps retreat down the corridor.

He's gone.

MORRIE: He?

TED: Yeah! That was a he.

MORRIE listens at the door.

Beat.

The manager. That was a bloke.

Beat.

Oh God, it's so exciting Morrie! The ad goes in this weekend. Sunday Times, News of the Screws, the Mail. I haven't put it in the Guardian. Don't want any bloody Guardian readers fucking things up. Yup! They won't be happy until we're all as miserable as they are. Yup! Saturday, Sunday! See the ad, ring up, watch the vid, sign up. A new beginning. (*He sits down again and stares at the camera.*)

MORRIE: Is Kath joining up? Kath and the kids?

TED: (*Smiling.*) I don't think so.

They exchange glances to say that the tape is rolling and TED starts more confidently.

Crime, pollution, noise, racial conflict, litter, war and TV filth…

To black.

Scene 2

The same room, but it is now dark outside. They have moved the camera to serve as a VCR to the television. MORRIE is sitting on the stage right side of the bed smoking. A tape is rewinding in the camera. TED is sitting with his back to him on the stage left side of the bed, wearing only his underpants, and reading the 'Daily Mail'.

TED: Ha! A Scotsman's won the Scottish Open. Good.
    That should keep the bastards quiet for a while.

Beat.

Tch. Tch! Tch!

Pause.

Huh! Tch, tch, tch.

MORRIE: What is it?

TED: You wouldn't believe it.

Beat.

Tch! Oh no! Tch. She's from Middlesborough.

MORRIE: What is it!?

TED: She fucked seven Greek waiters in ten days.

MORRIE: That's going some.

TED: Swordfish they're called. (*He chucks the paper aside in disgust.*) Fag!

MORRIE offers him a fag and lights it for him.

The Greeks eh? They peaked early. Your ancient Greek – Mathematics, geometry, astronomy, philosophy. They came up with the lot. But your modern Greek. Ha! What can he do, eh? Drive a taxi at ninety miles an hour in fucking flip-flops.

MORRIE: I don't like the Greeks, but they're not as bad as the Romans. We were teamed up with the Romans once of course, for ages, until we found out they was all homosexuals. I might have been Roman. There's a bit of Turkey what's named after me.

TED: What? Calvert?

MORRIE: Myopola. Which is Turkish for Calvert. A lot of English blood in that soil. We had thousands of men but

the Turks had machine guns. Kill a hundred men in a
minute. Two men – that's all you need. One to fire and
one to make the tea.

TED: War eh! We was lucky matey.

MORRIE: I would have liked to have been an anti-fascist
like my old dad.

TED: Nothing left worth fighting for matey. Take Europe.
We're fucked by being in Europe, but we're fucked if
we get out. That's the only choice we've got left – how
you wanna be fucked.

Beat.

What we doing now?

MORRIE: Rewinding. Lot of stuff there.

TED: Right, yeah. Too much?

MORRIE: Six hours. Can't get it all on one tape.

TED: Godda edit then?

MORRIE: You know all that scientific stuff about
whatsaname.

TED: Classical conditioning and operant conditioning.
That, that is the bloody key, Morrie!

MORRIE: Yeah? Well, it's clogged it up summat terrible.

TED: (*Realising he hasn't understood.*) A conditioned
response is the Pavlov's dog thing. Look, let's do it.
Look at me.

MORRIE: You what?

TED: Stand there and look at me.

TED winks at MORRIE. A big symbolic wink. MORRIE frowns.

Pause.

MORRIE: Why are you winking at me?

TED says nothing, but winks again. MORRIE says nothing. TED winks again. After a brief pause he winks again. This time, after a two second pause, he follows the wink with a slap.

Ow! What d'yer do that for?

TED winks at him again.

Why are you winking at me!?

TED slaps him across the face.

Ow!!

TED winks at him again. MORRIE backs off.

TED: Do you see?

MORRIE: See fucking what?!

TED: See what's happening, what's been established.

MORRIE: Every time you wink you follow it up with a slap.

TED: No, well yes, but that's not the important bit. What's important is I've conditioned your behaviour. When I wink now, you flinch. I've changed your behaviour. That's what's possible. Bloody hell, it's exciting isn't it?!

MORRIE: (*Quietly.*) Only 'cos you keep fucking hitting me!

TED: And Skinner proved that positive reinforcement using operant conditioning is twice as powerful as punishment. That's why love's so powerful and fucks us all up Morrie. Love is…it's…look all it is is mutual positive reinforcement. Yeah, you didn't know that did you? Skinner trained a pigeon to guide a nuclear missile. Bloody brilliant. In the Peru community constructive behaviour is rewarded whereas posing about like a twat is punished. Unlike in this country where the government pays you to sit on your arse all day tied to a dog, looking like a fucking muppet. Just think what we could do in a properly designed society.

Beat.

D'you know who I blame for the lousy, indolent attitude of today's youth. Eh? Woodwork teachers. Woodwork teachers, day in and day fucking out, teach our kids that it's perfectly acceptable to take three months to make one lousy cheeseboard. Three months!

Beat.

Japanese kids are turning out twenny cheeseboards every fucking hour! But you mention these ideas to your average Guardian reading aromatherapist wet fart of a Teddy Bear and they look at you as if you was Adolf bloody Hitler!

A key turns in the door. TED flattens himself against the wall ready to challenge whoever comes in. Nothing happens, except the catch on the lock is seen to turn. He listens at the door. The key turns again, and TED watches as the catch moves.

MORRIE: Good hair Hitler. Difficult obviously, but a very sensible compromise. A unique style. You'd think one of

those groups in the sixties would've picked up on it
wouldn't you?

TED turns the handle on the door, but it is locked.

TED: They've locked us in matey. Bloody hell. (*He tries the door again, and a third time. He inspects the lock.*)

MORRIE: Some barbers didn't like long hair, but I saw it as an opportunity. I instigated, what you might wanna call, a policy shift away from cutting towards the styling. I was the first barber in Walthamstow to do the mop, which of course, led on to the unisex thing.

TED: Will you listen to what I'm saying!?

MORRIE approaches TED as he stands by the door.

MORRIE: If you said 'unisex' to anyone, didn't matter where, you could be down West in a swanky bistro, but if you said the word 'unisex hairdressing' whoever it was you was talking to would say, 'Maurice Calvert,' and only then could the conversation continue.

TED: They've locked the fucking door!

MORRIE: (*Tries the door, turns and looks at TED.*) We've got a key. Unlock it.

TED: (*Picks up the key and goes to the door.*) No keyhole. There's no fucking hole! Stand back!

TED makes to kick the door down. He makes space for himself but MORRIE stands in front of him.

MORRIE: What have you done?

TED manhandles MORRIE out of the way and then he attacks the door and bashes it with his fists. During the following TED tries several strategies of opening the door – feet, shoulder, fists etc.

Hotel doors open inwards.

Beat.

I miss the shop. Personal visits. It's not the same. Cutting hair in a kitchen. With a shop you don't know who's gonna walk in. Who will walk through that door today?

TED: Shutup! For God's sake knock it on the head!

MORRIE: I had to listen to you.

TED picks up the trouser press, assesses it, and approaches the door intending to use it as a battering ram or axe.

Ted? Not a good idea.

TED puts the trouser press down, and sits on the bed, pulling his head down between his legs in frustration.

TED: (*Sighing.*) Sorry! (*He sits at the foot of the bed.*)

MORRIE: The Beatles' manager came in one day.

TED: Oh no! Not the fucking Beatles manager. You told me, you told me a thousand times!

MORRIE: They were nothing then, not at that time. Just another covers band. I'd seen them at the Palais, third on the bill, doing Elvis songs, but I spotted something in the big fellah…whatsis…

TED: (*Quickly.*) – Lennon, John Lennon.

MORRIE: – something not everyone could see, because, as you know I'm…

TED: (*Quickly.*) – psychic.

MORRIE: Psychic? Are you sure that's it.

TED: Yes! It means you get a feeling about things.

MORRIE: I do get a feeling about things.

TED: No Morrie, no!

MORRIE: I knew that night that The Beatles were going to be enormous, but only if they did one thing. Next day The Beatles manager walked into my shop out of the blue and I just said it, I gave it away, I said to him 'you wanna let those boys sing their own songs'. Next minute – whaddyaknow – Beatlemania.

Beat.

I'll keep my ideas to myself in future.

TED: Look mate, we're in a bit of a fix here…

MORRIE: You know those ocean-going tankers – the ones what take five miles to stop? Well, I've invented a system what lets 'em stop in five hundred yards. I'm not gonna tell nobody! Not after that Beatles business, oh no.

TED: You told me already!

MORRIE: Told you what?

TED: About the fucking tankers!

MORRIE: Well, keep it to yourself then.

TED: I've been trying to tell you, they've locked us in.

MORRIE: What the bleeding hell do you expect? You haven't paid the bill have you? You ain't got the money to pay me later on either have you? Eh?

TED: 'Course I have. When have I ever let you down?

MORRIE: Well, for a start…

TED: Alright!

Silence.

MORRIE: Someone's asked me to find them a shed. Did Mathew, you know knock it down, or did he like, take it to bits?

TED: What?!

MORRIE: The shed. What happened to the shed?

TED: Oh bloody hell!!

MORRIE: There you go. See. You're getting excited over nothing. Two people having a conversation about a shed and one of them starts steaming up.

TED: I am not steaming up! It's just…what are you talking about the shed for?

MORRIE: Someone's asked me to get them a shed – that's why!

TED: What about me? Eh? They've gone and bloody locked us in!

MORRIE: I'm here aint I?

TED grabs his own head and pulls it down into a severe head lock. MORRIE shuffles round and sits on the foot of the bed to be next to him.

Oh bloody hell, china! You're not going to do that one on me are you. You're like a bloody woman. Look I'm all yours. I brought me camera, me tapes, me acquired knowledge of cinematography. I could be shagging a

Mexican now. But no, I'm here 'cos my mate, my old china, rang up and asked me to be here. Remember when them lads from Shoreditch knifed you down the Regent's Canal, eh? I was there then. Did I run away? And Sandy, eh? I sorted you out with her didn't I. Put my head on the block there dint I? Specially since her dad was my 'eadmaster. Did my fucking life in, that did! My whole bloody life – education wise. Ted!

TED: (*Through snuffles from below.*) I know.

MORRIE: And the book, eh? Whose money was that?

TED: (*Coming up for air.*) I haven't forgotten.

MORRIE: I wouldn't have given you the money if I hadn't have thought it was a good book. I never met anyone who's written a book, apart from my old dad of course, but you'd expect that of him, wouldn't you? Only you could pick a bleeding astronaut as a hero. Ha, ha! What was it called again?

TED: Black Hole – the Return Journey of Starship Seven. With the seven in Roman numerals.

MORRIE: Mmm. I always wanted to know why they wanted to go there in the first place. I think you should have dealt with that.

TED: (*Angry.*) You've said that before!

MORRIE: Good descriptions in it. Anyone would think you'd actually lived in a black hole. Actually, could you do me a favour and take a thousand copies back up with you? I haven't been able to get in the lock up for nearly ten years now.

TED: Okay. Sorry, I had a go.

MORRIE: Everybody's got something wrong with 'em, Ted.

TED: Yeah?

MORRIE: 'Course.

There is a firm knock on the door. They stand and stare. A slip of paper is pushed under the door. TED stands and goes over, picks it up and reads it. Having read it he screws it up into a ball and throws it at the door, before sitting back down on the bed. MORRIE stands and goes over to the ball, picks it up, unscrews it and reads it, screws it up and throws it at the door.

That calls for a fag. (*He offers a cigarette to TED and lights it for him.*)

Are you gonna tell me? I can wait you know.

Pause.

TED: Two tapes eh?

MORRIE: You were very good china, for someone who's not a natural.

TED: I miss you Morrie. We've always had a laugh haven't we? And I don't make friends easily, I compare everybody to you and they always fall short. We're like brothers aren't we. Two cots side by side. Twins even.

MORRIE: Here we go.

TED sits on the stage right side of the bed. MORRIE presses play and goes to the mini-bar and gets a can of beer for TED and mixes himself another Bacardi and coke. The screen shows first a snow storm and then a girl in lingerie on a bed. The camera wobbles and refocusses. The girl rolls over and begins to undo her bra strap. At this moment TED cuts in and is talking to camera. 'Crime, pollution, noise, racial conflict, war and TV filth...'

TED: (*Stands and turns the video off.*) Who the fuck was that?

MORRIE: Katrina. That's the second one I did with her. People said it was too much like the first which, to be truthful, it was. There's only so much you can do you know, and once you've done it, you either do it again or stop.

TED: Yeah, yeah, yeah, but what I'm saying matey is we can't have that bit at the beginning of the tape. I'll end up looking like a bloody pervert!

MORRIE: This is the master. I'm gonna tape from this ain't I. Don't get so bleeding excited!

TED: (*Paces the room.*) I'm not getting excited!

MORRIE: (*Standing.*) You're going into one.

TED: (*Going into one.*) I am not going into one!

MORRIE: You're at top pitch!

TED: I am not at top pitch!! I need to look respectable. People won't sell up and join a radical socially engineered community if they think the leader is a fucking pervert. I've got to look clean, responsible, you know, nice.

MORRIE: No-one will see Katrina. So stop going into one.

TED: (*Calmly.*) I was not going into one. (*He sits on the end of the bed.*) Sorry.

MORRIE: You don't change do you?

TED: I've put everything into this. Money, time, energy, other people's money.

MORRIE starts the tape again and sits next to TED.

(*On tape.*) May, nineteen ninety-six. My son, by my first marriage, Mathew was halfway through knocking down a shed when he found this hard-backed novel.

At this point on the video TED leans over and picks up the copy of 'Walden Two' from the bed and in moving back into camera involuntarily crosses his legs revealing to the camera his bare feet. On seeing this TED stands, snatches the remote from MORRIE and approaches the video and stops it.

What in God's name was that?

MORRIE: What?

TED rewinds the video and plays it again, frame by frame, freeze framing on his naked foot.

TED: (*Pointing at the screen.*) That!

MORRIE: Your foot.

TED: My bare, fucking, nude foot! What are you?

MORRIE: You lifted your feet into shot. If you'd kept your feet –

TED: A stupid fucking cunt! (*He rewinds and has another look at it in real time.*)

MORRIE: If you play it at normal speed people will just think you're wearing sandals.

TED exits to the bathroom. We hear the taps running as TED washes his face.

TED: (*Off.*) A business suit, a good, expensive, business suit, dry cleaned yesterday, and bloody sandals. That is so Maurice Calvert!

MORRIE: (*Standing.*) Me?

TED: (*Off.*) You were doing some fancy camera work weren't you?

MORRIE: (*Advancing towards the bathroom.*) I wanted to sit down and have five minutes, but you wanted me to listen – even though I've heard this crap before.

TED slowly appears from the bathroom. MORRIE backs off slowly.

TED: Crap? Crap? It's all coming out now isn't it Morrie?

MORRIE: I don't mean crap crap. It's just a figure of speech.

TED: What are you doing here?

MORRIE: You asked me. I'm your china.

TED paces the room. MORRIE sits on the end of the bed.

TED: Do you think I'd make all the sacrifices I've had to make if I didn't think I hadn't not discovered possibly the holy grail of how to live. How we could all be?

MORRIE: People won't like all that control stuff.

TED: (*Intense.*) It's benevolent control! Morrie, do you think you're free now? You bought a lottery ticket today. Do you know why?

MORRIE: I could do with a small injection of cash. Small, or large.

61

TED: No. You bought a lottery ticket because you are permanently locked into a scientifically designed schedule of variable reinforcement. You didn't know that did you?

MORRIE: Never heard of it.

TED: You don't win every time, but every thirty times or so you win a tenner. That's a variable schedule of reinforcement. And the power of a variable schedule is that you never stop. That's Skinner. Misused. The most influential psychologist of the twentieth century.

MORRIE: What nobody's heard of.

TED: You're just like the blokes at work.

MORRIE: They taking the piss?

TED: More than that. Yeah. I got one of those written warnings. Disciplinary procedure. They sent me to see the Personnel Manager. Cunt.

MORRIE: What did he say?

TED: Made me pay the phone bill.

MORRIE: Ringing Peru every day?

Beat.

Well you should've thought of that earlier, you stupid prat!

TED: I've had to take time off. Research. Travel.

MORRIE: Oh no, a good job like that and you go AWOL?

TED: I told them Kath's mom had died, and we had to go to the funeral in Cerro de Pasco, Peru.

MORRIE: But Kath's mom lives in Melton Mowbray.

TED: Alive and bloody well. Anyhow, that cunt Personnel Manager's bloody secretary saw Kath in the vets.

MORRIE: What was Kath doing at the vets?

TED: The rabbit. The secretary says to her, 'Sorry to hear about your mother getting swept away in a flash flood.'

MORRIE: Bleeding hell. Kath must've gone into one? Did she?

TED: Dunno. I was in Peru.

MORRIE: She wouldn't be lost for words when you got back though.

TED: Worst day of my bloody life. But it'd been too much for her before that. She couldn't get the hang of the fax. I'd be at work talking to Peru and I'd give out my fax number. They try and send a fax to me at home and Kath would pick the bloody phone up. 'Course she doesn't speak Peruvian. Fucking embarrassing. She made me look unprofessional.

MORRIE: How is Kath?

TED: It's all over.

MORRIE: She get sick of all this? Huh! You're prone to obsessions aren't you. Obsessions that go bleeding wrong. Remember them whatsaname eggs!

TED: Pathogen-free eggs.

MORRIE: Bleeding hell, what a fuss that was. Pathogen-free eggs!

TED: Pathogen-free eggs from a pathogen-free flock.

63

MORRIE: Worked out about five bleeding quid an egg. God knows how much for half a dozen!

TED: Twenty nine pounds ninety-nine.

MORRIE: How much money did you piss down that one china?

TED: It's this bloody country! They don't like anything new. Leave it alone though Morrie, please!

MORRIE stands and starts pacing around, deep in thought. Two police sirens sound. It's cars arriving. They both listen to the arrival. TED turns the lights out, and closes the curtains. He then peeps out at the car park. MORRIE turns a lamp on and pushes a chair up against the door and jams the handle securely. TED watches but doesn't move.

What are you doing?

MORRIE: Locking us in.

TED: We're already locked in!

MORRIE: (*Puts the kettle on.*) Alright then I'm locking them out – until I've finished with you. Look the way I see it is – right, let's start at the beginning. There's three things what can be going on here. One – you've come across an old novel what has the holy grail of good living in it and you want me to help you make a video which shares this knowledge with the world and what helps you set up this whatsaname community.

TED: Utopian.

MORRIE: That's the one.

MORRIE finds an empty coke bottle and puts it on the coffee table.

(*Touching the coke bottle.*) Right, this is what we'll do. One. This is number one. The coke bottle means utopia, that's what all this is about. You, Ted Oswald, have got the answer what humanity has been scratching about for since Adam was just a twinkle in his dad's foliage. And I mean, truly, no messing you've got it. The answer. The coke bottle. Three.

TED: What about two?

MORRIE: I'm coming to two. Three. The pepper pot. (*He picks up the pepper pot and places it on the table.*) The pepper is, this is all a scam.

TED: No Morrie, no –

MORRIE: Give me a chance. A scam. Ad in the Sundays. A thousand people send in thirty quid. You're thirty grand ahead. That's the end of it.

TED: Please! You know me!

MORRIE: Yeah, I know. Which brings us to three.

TED: Two.

MORRIE: Thank you. Two. The fruit. (*He places the fruit bowl between the coke bottle and the pepper.*) Now two is the most difficult one from my point of view. In two, you've found an old novel in a shed in Chingford and you've gone off on one, like you do sometimes. You screw up in your job, nick a car and a load of company credit cards, fall out with a lovely girl, Kath, your wife, abandon your beautiful children, pull the plug on your marriage, and end up where the only people interested in you are the Old Bill. In two, basically you're off your trolley. You've got on the District Line, fallen asleep, and woken up at Barking.

Beat.

Now the difference between one and three, and number two, is that in one or three you can be a sane man, but in two – you've lost it.

TED: Which one do you think it is matey?

MORRIE: I know which one it is. That's not the point. You're the one who has to choose.

TED: I don't think I want to do this.

MORRIE: Well there's fuck all else to do before the Old Bill take you away.

MORRIE sits at the end of the bed. After a short while TED stands and starts circling the table. Having circled it once he sits back down.

TED: What's the pepper again?

MORRIE: Thirty grand scam.

Silence.

Look I'll just shift it down a bit so you can get a good look.

MORRIE stands and moves the coffee table down stage. He then sits down and they both continue to stare at the three objects in silence.

Cup of tea?

TED: Smashing. Have you got a ciggie?

MORRIE: 'Course. (*He gives him a fag and lights it for him. He lights one for himself too.*)

TED: Nice lighter that. I noticed it before.

MORRIE: Lovely innit. Nigerian bloke with one leg gave it to me.

TED: They've got their own barbers haven't they?

MORRIE: I know. Every time he hopped into the shop I nearly shit myself. I mean what could I do for him. I could shave it all off or go and buy him a hat. Anything in between I was scuppered. But he liked me. He got deported in the end. Turns out he was illegal. He was virtually running Hackney Council. Yeah. I liked him. It's made out of a man-eating tiger's tooth.

TED: Is that how he lost his leg?

MORRIE: Na! He was a good dancer. Yeah, watching him dance, you'd never know he only had one leg.

TED: Ha! You're a card Morrie.

Pause.

TED stands and goes over to the coffee table and stands before it thinking. He then sits down.

MORRIE: Not easy is it?

TED: I thought you said you knew which one it was?

MORRIE: I do! I'm saying it can't be easy for you.

TED: (*Sits.*) I can't do it.

MORRIE: Alright, we'll make it easier. Process of whatsaname.

TED: Elimination?

Pause.

It's not the pepper. (*He moves the pepper pot.*)

MORRIE: Shame. I was hoping it was a scam. I might have come in on that.

Pause.

TED: (*Standing.*) Lose the fruit!

MORRIE: I'm not touching it.

TED stands and approaches the coffee table.

Here's your tea.

MORRIE hands him his tea. TED is transfixed, staring at the fruit.

I'll tell you what I'll do, I'll make it harder, but in a sense easier. Take your cup of tea.

TED: Eh?

MORRIE: (*He picks an apple out of the bowl.*) I'm going to say something and if you think it's true, then you throw the tea in my face. Look, for example, if I say, 'This is an apple,' and you agree, you have to throw the tea in my face. Alright?

TED: (*Close to tears.*) I don't want to do this.

MORRIE: Here we go, pick up your tea. Come on!

TED, though looking down, picks up his tea. MORRIE puts the apple back in the bowl.

You ready? Right, here goes.

TED nods, reluctantly.

You, Edward Oswald of Ashby de la Zouch, are a sane man.

Pause.

If you think that's true, you have to throw your tea in my face.

They hold the position for a while. TED holding the cup of tea prone. He looks up and looks into MORRIE's eyes, looking for clues, direction, sympathy. Slowly he begins to cry, until there are big sobs, big gut-busting convulsions. MORRIE takes the coke bottle and puts it in the bin.

TED: (*Through sobs.*) I er... I don't know how it started Morrie.

MORRIE: Even I know that. It started with your Mathew knocking the shed down.

TED: Mathew knocks that shed down and finds that book. It's so bloody, incredibly exciting. To know that you have found treasure. (*Suddenly hopeful.*) This technology can change the way we live.

MORRIE: You couldn't change a light bulb Ted. You'd find a message on the ceiling.

Beat.

When did you fuck off with the car and the credit cards?

TED: Couple of weeks ago.

MORRIE: Did you get any cash?

TED: Bit.

MORRIE: And Kath's chucked you out?

TED: (*Looks out of the window and surveys the yard.*) Kath didn't want to take the kids out of school. Didn't want to give the kids the gift of a new life. That's when I got to thinking about what your old dad said.

MORRIE: I never had a dad! I made him up! You know
I did!

TED: I know, I know! What you said then. The perfect
murder. For years I've been thinking about it, and you
know what? It's duck's arse tight matey. Bloody hell it's
so exciting!

MORRIE: What are you talking about?

TED: The perfect murder plan.

MORRIE: What? The wino, the teeth, did he ever do it,
we'll never know?

TED: Yeah! I just need a blank piece of paper Morrie.
A new life. I'd be murdering me. I'd get a new life.

MORRIE: You gave your real name on the tape.

Pause.

TED: Fuck! You can edit that out, can't you?

MORRIE: 'Course.

TED: I've done it. The plan. Well, half of it. The easy bit.
The wino.

MORRIE: (*Starts backing away from him.*) Oh no.

TED: He's in the boot. My size. Perfect. No teeth. Dead.

*MORRIE has now backed almost into the bathroom
where he stops.*

You know me. I've started so I'll finish.

MORRIE: Who's the tramp Ted?

TED: I dunno. I found him under a tree. Near Quorn. The
Vale of Belvoir. Fucking about with one of his mates.

MORRIE: Did his mate see you?

TED: No, I was behind a wall, watching.

MORRIE: And what…you killed him?

TED: Yeah. His mate fucked off, this one fell asleep, and I suffocated him with a pillow, like you said.

MORRIE: You had a pillow with you?

TED: Yeah.

MORRIE: And his mate didn't see you?

TED: What if he did? He's a fucking wino. He wouldn't remember.

MORRIE: He might remember a man in a business suit wandering about in a field carrying a pillow.

TED: No, no. He didn't see me. No way.

TED opens the sash window. He looks at his car. He looks at the drop. He looks back into the room. Then he tears the sheets off the bed. Through the next he makes a blanket rope.

We've got to act quick now.

MORRIE: We?

TED: Okay. Okay. It's my thing I realise that, but I need your help matey. The next bit. Well, I'm not sure I'm up to it.

MORRIE: Kath. Little Ben, and Leslie.

TED: Yeah. I mean I'll do it. I just need a bidda moral support.

Beat.

They get back from Bridlington on Saturday night. We can't hang around – the wino's going off. He keeps farting. How long do they fart for?

MORRIE: What am I? I'm a barber.

TED: That's the sort of thing you know. If we get back to Ashby for four tomorrow we can stick the wino in the deep freeze. Kath gets back about six; do the business; get the wino out the freezer; string him up, then, I thought best leave it till night-time before we start chucking petrol about. Whaddyer think? Only you can help me Morrie.

MORRIE: You don't know when you've been helped. You brainless wanker.

TED: You're the only person I trust Morrie.

MORRIE: I tell you what I'll do. I'll do the only thing I've got left. I'll give you a haircut.

MORRIE moves to the video player, extracts the cassette from the player and throws it out the window into the kitchen bins. He does the same with the copy of 'Walden Two' and the papers. Looking out of the window he surveys the streets to assess the situation. At that moment the phone rings. TED drops the blankets and makes to answer the phone but MORRIE stops him.

I'll take that.

(*On the Phone.*) Hello…no, no, I'm not Edward Oswald… Yeah…yeah, he's here. We're locked in… Maurice Calvert… Hostage?… I'll ask him.

(*To TED.*) Ted, am I your hostage?

TED: What?

MORRIE: (*On the phone.*) No, I'm his friend... Don't do anything stupid? What do you mean by that? ...No?!... I don't believe it... I told you, I'm his friend... I won't!... I don't know, I'll ask him, hang on.

(*Puts his hand over the receiver and speaks to TED.*) Have you got a gun Ted?

TED: You what?

MORRIE: (*On the phone.*) No he hasn't... Me? What do I want a bleeding gun for?... I can assure you officer I have no intention of doing anything stupid... (*He slams the phone down on them.*)

TED: Police Morrie?

MORRIE: No, Interflora.

Phone rings again. They let it ring.

TED: Oh shit! (*He paces, he opens the window and looks out.*) Fifth bloody floor. Bugger! You could break your neck. Shit!

He tries the door again. But it is locked from the outside.

Phone rings under.

Bloody hell!

MORRIE: I spent the first fifteen years of my life wiping your bum, and bleeding hell I'm still doing it. (*He picks the phone up and slams it down.*)

TED: I just need a fresh start. A blank piece of paper.

MORRIE: Get your clothes off. When did you last have a trim?

TED: Two months ago.

MORRIE: Nice hot wash, and a scalp massage. I'll trim it if you like. Nothing else to do until the Old Bill make their move.

TED: They're supposed to think I'm in Exeter.

MORRIE: The credit cards Ted. Technology innit.

TED: They're clever aren't they?

MORRIE: (*Produces his scissors from a pocket.*) I've got my scissors. I'm mobile now, aint I. Take 'em everywhere.

TED gives up the idea of escape and takes his shirt off and goes over to check out the shower unit. MORRIE follows.

I've seen it all before. Come on.

TED: You couldn't find brothers closer. Fifteen years together in Barnado's.

MORRIE: Best years of my life.

TED: No secrets.

MORRIE turns on the shower and adjusts the temperature and tests it. TED strips completely and stands in the shower tray.

MORRIE: That's lovely. This'll wash all that shit out of your system china.

TED: Those bastards at Barnado's did a good job at the end of the day, you know when all's said and done. You a finalist in the world championships that time in Soho, and me, well you know, I've got six blokes under me at

Sumners and the lowest proportionate labour turnover percentage in the whole division. You don't get that by scratching your arse. Personality. Wife, and two kids. Yeah.

MORRIE begins spraying water all over TED who shuts his eyes and enjoys it.

MORRIE: Sit on the edge there china – I'll give you a shampoo.

TED sits on the edge of the shower tray. During the next MORRIE shampoos and rinses his hair.

I blame your old man. And I blame my dad too. Pair of cunts. Bleeding irresponsible. Couldn't happen nowadays. They'd have the government on their backs. If I'd have had a dad. Kaw! I could have done anything, diplomatic corps possibly. You too, in your own way. You've got a talent for...stubborn, sort of bulldog, dog at a bone persistency. 'Course you're unreliable, emotional, destructive, but that's cos you never had a dad neither. Why am I not like that then? Why am I not off me trolley like you?

TED: You made one up. Bloody superman dad you had. And girls. You always had the girls.

MORRIE: Kaw! They loved me. All that time in Barnado's, I never slept in my own bed.

TED: I used to like it in the morning when you came back to the dorm and told me about it matey.

MORRIE: Ha! I've never told you this, but I made a lot of those stories up.

TED: I guessed you had. Some of them.

MORRIE: Come and sit over here.

MORRIE dries his hair and guides him over to a chair. TED sits with the towel over his lap.

Now this is my scalp massage. Tell me if, at the end of it if you don't feel as randy as a teenager.

TED: Oh. Mmmmm.

MORRIE: That's it china. Let it go.

A police siren is heard approaching, a second one follows. They get louder and louder until they both pull up in the car park under the window.

I gave Andreas one of these one day. He's a bubb-Cypriot, though he hangs out with the Kurds. Do you know what the Turks call the Cypriots?

TED: No.

MORRIE: English bastards. We, Britain that is, used to have Turkey but we gave it to the Turks just to keep 'em quiet. The Turks don't like the Cypriots, nah! Mind you we don't like the Turks, and neither do the Cypriots. No-one likes the Turks much. The Greeks can't stand 'em, mind you they don't like the Greeks much either. I don't like the Greeks much, but they don't mind us. That's 'cos we gave them Cyprus. We could've given Cyprus to the Turks but we'd already given 'em Turkey earlier on, so we gave Cyprus to the Greeks just to wind 'em up – the Turks that is.

Telephone rings. MORRIE takes it.

(*On the phone.*) What now? ...he's having a haircut... me... I'm a barber...he'll come out in a minute...'cos he hasn't got any clothes on. (*He puts the phone down.*)

(*To TED.*) He said he wants to have a little chat with you. I mean, what do the police know about the art of conversation?

Andreas, the contract killer, he come round one day, been on manoeuvres with his guerrilla movement, the Kurdish lot. I give him my special, this. Next day half the Pesh Merga guerillas in Stoke Newington come round wanting scalp massages. They're all international socialists too, though to be honest their sphere of influence don't go much beyond Manor House. There you go. (*He finishes the scalp massage.*)

TED: Kaw! That was smashing.

MORRIE: Now just a bit of a trim.

TED: What about your hands?

MORRIE: I'll stay clear of the ears. Stick to the wide open spaces.

TED: I wish I could help you out Morrie, you know, if ever –

MORRIE: You stood in the witness box that time.

TED: All I said was – what did I say exactly? 'Your honour, I cannot envisage a situation where Mr Calvert would do such a disgusting thing.' It was nothing. Just a white lie.

MORRIE: I got my problems an' all you know. This Bob who's moved into my maisonette. The one who saws. He thinks I'm Ralph.

TED: You said. Yeah, tell me.

MORRIE: It all started when Ralph started looking like me. Ralph's nose started to shrink and then his ears got wider, and he even got a scar on his neck like mine from when I was hanged in a previous existence. Then Bob stops me in the garage, I was getting my electricity key done, and he says, 'Ralph?' I said, 'I'm not Ralph, I'm Morrie.' Now this Bob spends his afternoons in my kitchen 'cos he thinks I'm Ralph. And he saws everything up. If it's made of wood he'll saw it in half.

Telephone rings.

(*On the phone.*) Yeah?… There's a chair against the door…yeah, we're coming out now… No, no, don't do that…he's coming out. Give us a minute. (*Phone down.*) They were gonna break your door down.

TED: Tch! We got a lot done today.

MORRIE: Yeah. It'll be prison.

TED: You know what they don't like? I've had a dream, that's what I've done, that's what they bloody well can't handle!

MORRIE: You killed a man.

TED: A wino Morrie. A stinking, filthy, pickled piece of useless scum. I mean, I know I shouldn't have done it, now, I've come round to that, but I mean, it's not as if I've knocked off anyone of note is it? You know, a bloke with a wife and kids, or a midwife, I don't know, Galileo or someone who's actually, you know, making some sort of contribution to this fucking sick society.

Pause.

I shouldn't have killed him should I. Shit! You know, if you lived up in Ashby I – shit! How long will I get? Murder.

MORRIE: Dunno. Five years maybe.

TED: (*Disappointed.*) Is that all? What is this country coming to?! You kill someone in cold blood, premeditated murder, and all you get is five years!

The trim ends.

MORRIE: There we go. That looks a lot neater.

TED stands and goes to the bathroom and looks in the mirror.

Now then. Small matter of the agreed sum.

TED: (*Off.*) Looks good.

(*Comes back in.*) Fifty quid?

MORRIE: Fifty. Cash.

TED goes into his jacket pocket and picks out his wallet. He looks through various compartments before producing five ten pound notes, which he gives to MORRIE who counts them.

Why didn't you pay for the room with this?

TED: That was your money, all along.

MORRIE starts packing the video away. A sledgehammer smashes through the door revealing its chipboard and veneer structure. Immediately MORRIE's there and shouts through the hole.

MORRIE: Stop, we're coming out! He's coming out. He's unarmed.

TED goes over to inspect the damage.

POLICEMAN: (*Voice off, through megaphone.*) Walk slowly into the hall! With your hands in the air!

MORRIE: (*Head poking through the hole.*) Alright, alright, keep your hair on, he's coming out.

TED: You see Morrie, I told you – veneer.

MORRIE: Ready?

TED: Don't tell Kath eh, you know, about…?

MORRIE: What? You planning to kill her?

TED: Yeah. That wouldn't go down too well.

MORRIE: 'Course not.

TED: Look on the bright side eh? They've got a good library service, inside haven't they, won't be too bad as long as I don't have to share a cell with a nutter. I'm not coming here again. Forty quid! You go to France. They have like motels, yeah, on the péage, their motorways? Guess how much for a family room? That's me, Kath, Ben and Leslie all in one room.
Roof, bed, secure parking. Go on, guess!

MORRIE: (*Angry.*) I told you, I don't have a car. Haven't you been listening!?

TED: One hundred and fifty francs. Fifteen quid. That wouldn't get you two slices of fried bread here. It's this country Morrie, that's what it is.

Okay. I'll go first.

(*Shouting.*) We're coming out! We're not armed. Repeat, no arms!

TED unlocks the door and looks out. He sticks his head back in.

Fucking hell! There's hundreds of them.

POLICEMAN: (*Voice off, through megaphone.*) Walk slowly! Put your hands in the air!

TED walks out with one hand in the air, the other holding his suit.

TED: (*Off.*) I'm Ted Oswald.

POLICEMAN: (*Off.*) Put that down! Slowly! Now, both arms in the air! Now!

TED: (*Standing in the doorway.*) Alright, alright. My mate here, he's got nothing to do with it. Eh, Morrie! Come on!

(*To the Police.*) You've made a bit of a mess of this door. There was never any need for that you know.

TED moves forward, off. MORRIE contemplates the room, and turns the light out.

To black.

The End.